John Hancock

History Maker Bios

Candice Ransom

LERNER PUBLICATIONS COMPANY • MINNEAPOLIS

To Joni, who loves clothes!

Illustrations by Tim Parlin

Text copyright © 2005 by Candice Ransom
Illustrations copyright © 2005 by Lerner Publications Company

Lerner Publications Company
A division of Lerner Publishing Group
241 First Avenue North
Minneapolis, MN 55401 U.S.A.

Website address: www.lernerbooks.com

Library of Congress Cataloging-in-Publication Data

Ransom, Candice F., 1952–
    John Hancock / by Candice Ransom.
        p.   cm. — (History maker bios)
    Includes bibliographical references and index.
    ISBN: 0–8225–1547–4 (lib. bdg. : alk. paper)
    1. Hancock, John, 1737–1793—Juvenile literature. 2. Statesmen—United States—Biography—Juvenile literature. 3. United States. Declaration of Independence—Signers—Biography—Juvenile literature. 4. United States—History—Revolution, 1775–1783—Juvenile literature. 5. United States. Continental Congress—Biography—Juvenile literature. 6. Governors—Massachusetts—Biography—Juvenile literature. I. Title. II. Series.
    E302.6.H23R36 2005
    973.3'092—dc22   2004002388

Manufactured in the United States of America
1 2 3 4 5 6 – JR – 10 09 08 07 06 05

TABLE OF CONTENTS

INTRODUCTION

John Hancock is best known for signing the Declaration of Independence. His large, fancy signature stands out among the other names.

John enjoyed fine clothes, wine, and food. Some people thought John Hancock *only* cared about money. But they were wrong. When the British king unfairly taxed Americans, John joined the colonists who were against the king's laws. He risked his life to help America become free.

John Hancock wrote fancy so people would notice him. Yet he is probably the least known of the American patriots.

This is his story.

1 RAGS TO RICHES

On January 12, 1737, a baby boy was born in Braintree, Massachusetts. He was given his father's and grandfather's name, John Hancock.

John's father and grandfather were both ministers. They expected little John to follow in their footsteps. He would go to Harvard College and become a minister too.

Braintree was a farming village. Most boys had to milk cows, feed the hogs, chop firewood, haul water, and work in the garden. John's father didn't own a farm, so John didn't have to do farm chores.

John tagged along with John Adams and the Quincy brothers, Edmund and Samuel. The older boys didn't like John. They thought he complained too much. John wished the boys liked him.

In the 1700s, many boys lived and worked on farms like this one.

In 1742, when John was five, he started going to Mrs. Belcher's country school. Along with John Adams and the Quincy brothers, John learned reading, writing, and arithmetic. Later, John would be expected to attend the local grammar school and then go on to Harvard.

But John's father died in 1744, when John was just seven. Suddenly, the Hancock family was poor. John, his mother, his older sister, Mary, and younger brother, Ebenezer, had no place to live.

Classes were small in country schools, and the students all met in one room.

John's grandfather let them move into his big house in Lexington, Massachusetts. Reverend Hancock was eager to start training John to be a minister.

John's Uncle Thomas had other ideas. He came to Lexington from Boston to talk to John's mother.

THOMAS HANCOCK

Thomas Hancock (right) was one of the richest men in the American colonies. He left home at the age of fourteen to seek his fortune. Starting with a small store, his business grew into the House of Hancock. His fleet of ships carried all types of goods between Boston and London, England. People said if you couldn't find what you wanted at Hancock's, he would get it for you.

Thomas and his wife, Lydia, had no children. He wanted to adopt John and teach him the family business. John's mother agreed and told John to pack his belongings.

John stared at his uncle's gold-trimmed carriage, which was pulled by four horses. His uncle's four servants were dressed in fine uniforms. John felt drab in his homemade suit.

He admired his uncle's velvet suit, lace-trimmed shirt, silver shoe buckles, and powdered wig. He wondered about this rich uncle who was taking him away.

The horses hurried through the countryside and into the city of Boston. At the top of Beacon Hill was a large green lawn called the Common. Cows and sheep grazed on the grass.

People and animals shared the Common.

Thomas Hancock's home was one of the largest houses in Boston.

The coach stopped before the grandest house John had ever seen. The three-story, stone mansion had fifty-three windows of the finest English glass. Formal gardens, an orchard, and big, shady trees surrounded the grounds.

Inside, Aunt Lydia welcomed him warmly. New clothes waited for John in his new room. Soon John was dressed in velvet pants, a fancy shirt with lace trim, and shoes with shiny silver buckles.

John couldn't believe he was actually living in this amazing place. He liked it! He hoped he would make new friends here.

2 BOSTON'S PRINCE

At his new school, John sharpened his turkey-feather quill pen, then dipped the point into the ink pot. He and his classmates practiced handwriting at the end of every day. John loved writing his name different ways.

Boston Public Latin School was a lot harder than Mrs. Belcher's school. John studied Latin and Greek four days a week plus a half day on Saturday.

John longed for friends. But the other boys were jealous of John's wealth. John was driven to school in his uncle's carriage. Servants opened the door for him and carried his books.

John spent up to ten hours each day studying at Boston Public Latin School (BUILDING ON THE RIGHT).

When John wasn't studying, his uncle took him to Boston Harbor. John loved seeing the ships at the docks.

Some of the ships belonged to his uncle. Inside the House of Hancock, clerks kept track of the company's bills.

John knew his uncle wanted him to take over the family business someday. He believed his uncle was the king of Boston. That meant he must be the prince of Boston!

Thomas Hancock's ships sailed from Boston Harbor.

Harvard College opened in 1636 — more than one hundred years before John went to school there.

In 1750, thirteen-year-old John entered Harvard College. He was the second youngest in his class of twenty students.

John studied math, geometry, the Bible, Latin, Greek, speech, and writing. At Harvard, John had more friends. His friend Samuel Quincy was also there.

After graduating from Harvard in 1754, John went to work for his uncle. He carefully copied letters in his fancy handwriting and learned about the business of buying and selling goods.

In August 1764, Thomas Hancock died. He left his big house, ships, shops, and property to his twenty-seven-year-old nephew. John was one of the richest men in America. Suddenly, Boston's prince was Boston's king.

John settled into his new role. He ordered more beautiful clothes from London. Like other important men, he covered his brown hair with powdered wigs.

John enjoyed being fashionable, but he also spent long hours at his job. More than a thousand people worked for him. Those people depended on him.

Making money wasn't easy. It became harder in 1765. The British government passed a law called the Stamp Act. The law made people in America pay for a official stamp on all newspapers, legal papers, and even playing cards. Many Americans were against the law.

The Stamp Act made colonists pay for stamps like this one.

At that time, Britain ruled the American colonies. John had always been loyal to Great Britain and King George III. But this law made him angry too. He refused to pay the tax.

Trouble was brewing in the colonies. Samuel Adams, John Adams's cousin, and others formed a group called the Sons of Liberty.

"No Taxation without Representation"

Americans used this saying to describe why they disagreed with the tax laws of King George III (*below right*). Colonists did not have a say in Parliament, where Britain's laws are made. No one spoke up for what the colonists wanted. They got angry when Britain decided to tax them without their permission.

The Sons of Liberty wanted the Stamp Act repealed, or ended. They talked to people on the streets, in taverns, and in meetings. They attacked stamp agents, the people who sold the stamps and collected the tax money.

To succeed, the Sons of Liberty needed help from all types of Americans. Samuel Adams talked to John. He knew that if a man as rich and influential as John decided to support the Sons of Liberty, other men and women would do the same.

Colonists rally to oppose the Stamp Act.

At first, John joined the Sons of Liberty to protect himself and his property from the protests and fighting that had broken out in Boston. He met many patriots—colonists who were against the king's laws. As time went on, they became John's new friends.

In May 1766, one of John's ships brought news. Parliament, the group that made laws for Britain and the American colonies, had repealed the Stamp Act. The Sons of Liberty had done it! When John made the announcement, the people of Boston thought he had helped end the law. John threw the biggest party Boston had ever seen, with fireworks and kegs of wine.

Everyone liked him! That was more important to John than worrying about what the king of England thought.

3 LOYALIST TO PATRIOT

One cold February night in 1767, a fire burned more than twenty houses. Fifty families were left homeless. The next day, John rode to the disaster area. He gave away money, firewood, and food. Helping people made John feel good.

John was a popular man. The people of Boston elected him as one of five city leaders. At meetings, the leaders discussed the city's funds, schools, streets, and police force.

Late that summer, Parliament passed a set of laws called the Townshend Acts. The laws forced colonists to pay new taxes on paper, lead, glass, paint, and tea. Men called customs agents collected the taxes. Americans were angrier than ever. Why should they pay taxes to the king when they had no one to speak for them in Parliament?

LOYALISTS

Colonists who were loyal to King George called themselves Loyalists. (Patriots called them Tories.) Even though they didn't always agree with the king's policies, they did not want to rebel against Britain. When the American Revolution began, many Loyalists fought alongside the British.

John was angry too. When his ship, the *Lydia,* sailed into Boston Harbor in 1768, two customs agents came to check the ship. John blocked their way. John's bold stand made him a hero.

But the king was not pleased. Soon after, the *Liberty,* another of John's ships, arrived in the harbor. Customs agents boarded the ship and took it for the British government.

John knew he was making enemies by siding with the patriots. He was still a businessman and never meant to make trouble. But the people of Boston liked him better as a hero for the patriots.

John was a busy patriot, but he worked hard to make sure his business did well too.

The king had had enough of these troublemaking colonists. In October 1768, he sent troops to force the people in Boston to obey the laws. The troops camped and marched on the Common.

The Sons of Liberty walked the streets, stirring up protests against the British. On March 5, 1770, angry colonists argued with British soldiers. A fight broke out, and the soldiers fired their guns at the crowd. When it was over, five colonists lay dead. The event was called the Boston Massacre.

Crispus Attucks (CENTER) was one of the colonists killed in the Boston Massacre.

The sailors on John's ships brought good news from Britain.

In Britain, Parliament stopped taxing most items included in the Townshend Acts. Once more, the news arrived on one of John's ships. Once more, the people believed John helped end the law. They reelected him as a city leader and gave him 511 votes out of 513.

The king did not want John to give the rebels any more help. He tried to win John over to his side by making John leader of a group of soldiers called the Corps of Cadets. John and his soldiers were to stop riots. John was thrilled to have a military job.

In 1773, colonists grumbled over the Tea Act, a new tax on British tea. In protest, many colonists stopped drinking British tea. John and other members of the Sons of Liberty demanded that British tea ships in Boston Harbor be sent back to Britain. The ships' captains refused to leave.

The Sons of Liberty decided to solve the problem their own way. On the night of December 16, 1773, nearly fifty men dressed as Mohawk Indians sneaked onto the British tea ships. With axes, they split open chests of tea and dumped the tea into the dark water.

Dressed as Mohawk Indians, the Sons of Liberty threw British tea from ships into the water. This event became known as the Boston Tea Party.

John never said that he knew anything about the event, called the Boston Tea Party. The king was furious. Where was John's Corps of Cadets while the tea was being dumped into the harbor?

In February 1774, King George charged John Hancock and Samuel Adams with treason. The king had officially named them enemies of the British government. If caught and found guilty, they could be hanged.

Samuel Adams organized many protests against the British, including the Boston Tea Party.

Old South Meeting House was the biggest building in colonial Boston.

Unafraid, John gave a bold speech on the fourth anniversary of the Boston Massacre, March 5, 1774. He dressed in one of his fine velvet suits and spoke to a large crowd at Old South Meeting House in Boston. He announced that he could no longer support the unfair laws of King George.

He told Massachusetts to fight for liberty. If the other colonies joined Massachusetts, America could become a free nation. As John left the meeting house, the crowd cheered in approval.

4 FIRST SIGNER

After the Boston Tea Party, King George closed Boston Harbor and sent more troops across the Atlantic. The colonists had to do something. Representatives, people chosen to speak for the different colonies, decided to meet.

The representatives met in September 1774 in Philadelphia, Pennsylvania. At this meeting, called the First Continental Congress, they wrote up their complaints and sent them to King George.

At the same time, the people in Massachusetts set up their own government. A group of 250 people met and elected John as leader of Massachusetts. John was glad people had that much faith in him.

The First Continental Congress met in Carpenter's Hall in Philadelphia, Pennsylvania, in September 1774.

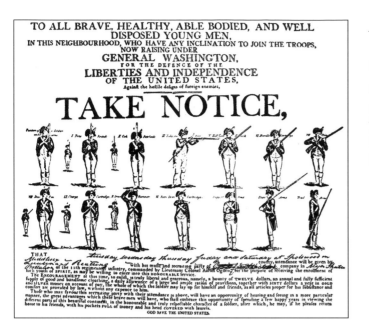

This poster calls for brave young men to join the fight for American independence.

In his new role, John and other leaders called for an army of "minutemen." These volunteers would be ready to fight on short notice. Each soldier was given a gun and bullets. To pay for the supplies, John raised money from other business owners and generously gave his own money.

While John was away meeting with other patriots, British forces attacked near his home. John worried about his Aunt Lydia and Dolly Quincy, the beautiful woman he was courting. He sent them to stay at his grandfather's house in Lexington.

In April 1775, John left with Samuel Adams for Lexington. They feared that the king would soon call for their arrest. Sure enough, British general Thomas Gage ordered his troops to capture the two men.

The British also planned a big attack. A man named Paul Revere learned about the plans. He rode his horse overnight to warn the minutemen. He also warned John and Samuel that they were in danger. John and Samuel escaped in John's carriage.

On Paul Revere's famous ride, he warned that the British were coming.

The next morning, Gage's troops and the minutemen fought in Lexington. The American Revolution had begun.

John and Samuel Adams headed to Philadelphia for the Second Continental Congress. In Philadelphia, John was elected president of the Congress. John proudly sat in the president's chair as members voted to organize and train a national army.

"THE SHOT HEARD 'ROUND THE WORLD" General Gage and his seven hundred soldiers planned to capture John Hancock and Samuel Adams in Lexington. They also wanted the patriots' supply of bullets and guns in nearby Concord. But after Paul Revere's warning, seventy minutemen were waiting when the British arrived. No one knows what happened next, but someone fired a shot. The first shot in Lexington was indeed heard around the world. It began the American Revolution.

John was sure he would be chosen to lead the colonies' Continental Army. He was ready to accept the honor when George Washington was picked instead!

As president of Congress, John did fill an important role. He signed orders for guns, food, and blankets for Washington's men. All that practicing in school had paid off. People noticed his signature.

George Washington (STANDING RIGHT) agreed to lead the Continental Army.

Dolly and John married on August 28, 1775.

Before settling into his new job, John married Dolly Quincy. While John and Dolly were in Philadelphia, John's aunt Lydia died. John was sad to lose the woman who had been like a second mother to him.

In 1776, the colonies decided to declare independence from Britain. John asked Thomas Jefferson, Benjamin Franklin, John Adams, Roger Sherman, and Robert Livingston to write the document.

On July 4, 1776, Congress approved
the Declaration of Independence and ended
its meeting. Alone except for Secretary of
Congress Charles Thomson, John picked
up his quill pen and signed his name
in large, elegant script.

John Hancock's signature looked as
important as America's most important
document. His name stood for freedom.

*John signed the
Declaration of
Independence
in large letters
to show King George
that he believed in
American freedom.*

5 KING OF MASSACHUSETTS

Declaring independence didn't solve America's problems with Britain. King George would not give up his colonies so easily. In the summer of 1776, British troops captured New York City. The patriots were in danger of losing the war.

Homesick, John and Dolly left Philadelphia and traveled to Boston. As thanks for his gifts to the city, the people of Boston gave John a yellow carriage. John loved riding around the city in it with his Corps of Cadets marching in front and behind.

In 1777, Dolly gave birth to a little girl named Lydia. Sadly, Lydia died less than a year later. John was overjoyed when a son was born in 1778. John admired George Washington so much that he named his son after him—(and himself)—John George Washington Hancock. Secretly, John still longed to be an officer in George Washington's army.

John greatly respected George Washington.

The French navy helped fight for America's independence.

In 1778, the French navy arrived to help the Americans. Military leaders from both countries planned to attack British troops in New York City and Newport, Rhode Island. Best of all, John would lead six thousand men at the Newport battle.

But first John needed the right clothes. While the other generals figured out how to fight the British, John spent three weeks packing his trunks. Instead of planning battles, John planned how his servants would race back home to Boston with his dirty clothes and bring back clean ones.

But the battle wasn't very nice. Booming cannons gave John a headache. He forgot a favorite pair of boots, he couldn't sleep, and it rained the whole time. His troops lost the battle, and John went home.

Back in Boston, John did what he did best—throw parties. He and Dolly entertained the officers from the French ships. One memorable breakfast for 120 sent Dolly Hancock scurrying for twelve pounds of butter, gallons of milk, and all the cake she could borrow from neighbors.

John and Dolly enjoyed giving parties.

John spent his own money on these fancy meals. Although he wasn't a very good general, he made the French officers feel welcome. It was an important job. The Americans needed France's help if they were going to win the war.

The people of Massachusetts still loved John. In 1780, they elected him governor. He won 11,000 votes out of 12,281.

On October 25, 1780, John dressed in a red jacket with gold trim and a white vest. He climbed into his yellow carriage. Church bells rang, and cheering crowds called his name. John was His Excellency, the governor!

After John was elected governor, his Boston home was busier than ever.

Colonists in each state paid taxes with money printed for only their state.

   As governor, John had to help find ways to pay for the American Revolution. The war ended with an American victory at Yorktown, Virginia, in 1781. John raised and lowered taxes. He wrote laws and passed bills, signing with his famous signature.

   John was glad the people of Massachusetts liked him. But he grew tired of being governor. He suffered from gout, a painful condition that caused swollen joints. He was often in a wheelchair, and some days he could barely write his name.

In 1789, Americans were ready to choose a president. George Washington seemed sure to win the most votes. The person who won second place would become vice president. Some people thought John would be a good vice president. But other voters worried that he was too sick for the job. He lost to his old friend John Adams.

John was elected governor nine times. The voters wanted him to be their governor forever.

John Adams finished in second place in America's first presidential election. He became the first vice president.

But John's health continued to fail. By September 1793, he was unable to stand or read his speeches. On Tuesday, October 8, 1793, John Hancock died. He was fifty-six years old.

"HANCOCK IS DEAD" the *Boston Independent Chronicle* announced in big, bold letters. The newspaper headline was just right for a man who signed his name in big, bold letters.

John Hancock had always wanted friends. He spent his life helping people and the American cause for freedom. At his death, he had more friends than he could count.

TIMELINE

JOHN HANCOCK WAS BORN
ON JANUARY 12, 1737.

In the year . . .

1744	John's father died. he moved to Boston to live with his uncle, Thomas Hancock.	Age 7
1754	he graduated from Harvard.	
1764	his uncle, Thomas Hancock, died. he inherited the House of Hancock.	Age 27
1765	he protested the Stamp Act.	
1766	he joined the Sons of Liberty.	
1770	the Boston Massacre took place on March 5.	
1774	he gave his famous speech after the Boston Tea Party. the American Revolution began on April 19.	Age 37
1775	he was elected president of the Continental Congress. he married Dolly Quincy.	
1776	he signed the Declaration of Independence on July 4. his daughter, Lydia, was born.	Age 39
1777	his daughter died.	
1778	he lost the battle at Newport, Rhode Island. his son, John George Washington, was born.	
1780	he was elected the first governor of Massachusetts.	Age 43
1789	the first president of the United States was elected.	
1793	he died in Boston on October 8.	Age 56

LEGENDS OF THE SIGNING

The most important paper John signed was the Declaration of Independence. Paintings show many people watching as John dipped his quill in ink. In 1819, Thomas Jefferson recalled that all members of the Continental Congress but one had seen John sign.

Some people said that after John finished his large, fancy script, he stated, "There, I guess King George will be able to read that!" Others reported that John said, "There! John Bull [the British] can read my name without spectacles and may now double his reward of 500 pounds for my head. That is my defiance."

In truth, only the secretary of Congress witnessed John's signature. The others had left and did not sign until weeks later. For nearly a month, John Hancock's was the only name on the document that declared America a free nation.

John signed the Declaration of Independence with a quill pen similar to this one.

FURTHER READING

Dunnahoo, Terry. *Boston's Freedom Trail.* **New York: Dillon Press, 1994.** Photos and descriptions of the historic monuments along Boston's Freedom Trail.

Fradin, Dennis Brindell. *The Signers: The Fifty-six Stories behind the Declaration of Independence.* **New York: Walker, 2002.** Brief illustrated biographies of all signers of the Declaration of Independence, with additional background information about patriot activities in each of the thirteen colonies.

Fritz, Jean. *Why Don't You Get a Horse, Sam Adams?* **New York: Putnam, 1974.** A lively illustrated biography about the passionate patriot Samuel Adams.

Fritz, Jean. *Will You Sign Here, John Hancock?* **New York: Putnam, 1976.** A humorous account of the life of John Hancock, with illustrations.

King, David. *Lexington and Concord.* **New York: Twenty-first Century Books, 1997.** A photo-illustrated description of how the American Revolution began and what happened in the war's first battle.

Ransom, Candice F. *George Washington.* **Minneapolis: Lerner Publications Company, 2002.** A colorful biography about the first president of the United States.

Sutcliffe, Jane. *Paul Revere.* **Minneapolis: Lerner Publications Company, 2002.** A lively biography of one of the most famous patriots of the American Revolution.

Warner, J.F. *Massachusetts.* **Minneapolis: Lerner Publications Company, 2002.** An overview of the state's history, geography, government and economy, people, famous citizens, and landmarks, illustrated with many photos.

WEBSITES

The Declaration of Independence
<www.archives.gov/national_archives_experience/
declaration.html> This website contains a photo image of
this document and links to additional resources.

Signers of the Declaration of Independence
<www.ushistory.org/declaration/signers/hancock.htm>
This website has information on John Hancock. Short
biographies are provided for each of the fifty-six signers of
the Declaration of Independence.

SELECT BIBLIOGRAPHY

Dershowitz, Alan M. *America Declares Independence.* New
York: John Wiley & Sons, 2003.

Langguth, A. J. *Patriots: The Men Who Started the
American Revolution.* New York: Simon & Schuster,
1988.

McCullough, David. *John Adams.* New York: Simon &
Schuster, 2001.

Morris, Jerry. *The Boston Globe Guide to Boston.* Old
Saybrook, CT: Globe Pequot Press, 1999.

Unger, Harlow Giles. *John Hancock: Merchant King and
American Patriot.* New York: John Wiley & Sons, 2000.

Wilson, Susan. *Literary Trail of Greater Boston.* Boston:
Houghton Mifflin, 2000.

INDEX

Acknowledgments

For photographs and artwork: © historypictures.com, pp. 4, 15, 24; The Granger Collection, New York, pp. 7, 8, 9, 33, 38, 39; Library of Congress, pp. 10 (LC-USZ62-75184), 11 (LC-USZ62-96232), 18 (LC-USZ61-536), 25 (LC-USZC4-523), 26 (LC-D416-256), 34 (LC-USZ62-96235), 35 (LC-USZ62-14), 40 (LC-USZ62-96218), 42 (LC-USZ62-126308); © Brown Brothers, pp. 14, 16; © North Wind Picture Archives, p.17; Independent Picture Service, pp. 22, 29; National Archives, pp. 23 (W&C #2), 30 (W&C #70); Cornell University Library, Making of America Digital Collection, p. 27; Painting by Charles Hoffbauer, courtesy of New England Mutual Life Insurance, Boston, Massachusetts, p. 31; Independence National Historical Park, p. 37; © James Marrinan, p. 41; Courtesy National Park Service, Museum Management Program and Morristown National Historical Park, p. 45. Front cover: © Bettmann/CORBIS. Back cover: Cornell University Library, Making of America Digital Collection.
For quoted material: pp. 43, 45, Harlow Giles Unger, *John Hancock: Merchant King and American Patriot* (New York: John Wiley & Sons, 2000).